Vegan Slow Cooker Cookbook:

Easy Slow Cooker Vegan Recipes to follow

Charlie Mason

CONTENTS

Introduction

The following chapters will discuss some of the many different ways you can prepare a vegan style meal or snacks that your friends and family are sure to enjoy. With 31 recipes, you can try a different one every single day of the month.

You will discover how important it is to watch what you eat and how it's prepared. The slow cooker provides you with the extra time that you can spend on the important things involved with your busy lifestyle. It will let your family know how much you care by offering such tasty meals, snacks, and desserts.

Choosing the vegan way of eating means you will receive nutritional benefits from vegetables, fresh fruits, nuts, beans, whole grains, and soy products. These are some of those benefits and how your health can be affected by making <u>good</u> food choices:

- **Antioxidants**: With this addition, you can protect your body against several types of cancer.

- **Protein**: Red meat is not necessarily the healthiest choice for protein. As a vegan, lentils, nuts, peas, beans, and soy products provide this resource without the health issues.

- **Carbohydrates**: Your body will tend to burn your muscle tissue if you don't eat plenty of carbs.

- **Vitamin C**: The C vitamin works as an antioxidant and helps your bruises heal faster and keeps your gums healthy.

- **Fiber**: The vegans experience better bowel movements with the increased high fiber in veggies and fruits.

- **Reduced Saturated Fats**: Without the meats and dairy products, these levels are lowered immensely.

- **Magnesium**: With the assistance of magnesium, calcium is better absorbed. It is found in dark leafy greens, seeds, and nuts.

- **Potassium**: Acidity and water are balanced by potassium which also leads to a reduction in cancer and cardiovascular diseases.

There are plenty of books on this subject on the market, thanks again for choosing this one! Every effort was made to ensure it is full of as much useful information as possible. Please enjoy!

CHAPTER 1

Breakfast Delights

Beginning every morning with a healthy start can commence with a healthy breakfast bar, a bowl of oatmeal, or a plate of tasty vegan style eggs. These are just a few that will get you up and motivated.

Blueberry – Coconut Breakfast Quinoa

This combination of blueberry and coconut seems to wake up the quinoa to get your day headed in the right direction.

Ingredients
2 c. frozen blueberries
¼ c. sweetened/unsweetened shredded coconut
1 tbsp. molasses
1 can (13.5 oz.) coconut milk
¼ cup of each:
   -Toasted coconut
   -Chopped almonds
¾ c. quinoa

Instructions

1. Rinse the quinoa to remove its bitterness. Once rinsed, toss it into the slow cooker.
2. Sprinkle the coconut over the top with a drizzle of molasses.

3. Open and stir the can of milk until it is smooth. Empty it into the cooker, gently stirring. Set the cooker on high for 1 ½ - 2 hours or low for 3 hours.
4. Scoop out the tasty breakfast into the bowls topping with about one tablespoon of chopped almonds and some of the blueberries.

Yields: 4 Servings

Cinnamon Apple Oatmeal

You will wonder why you have not tried this before. It is so tasty, in particular on a cold weekend. Not only will it warm your insides, but it will also send a tantalizing aroma throughout your home!

Ingredients
2 sliced apples
1/3 c. maple syrup or to your liking
1 tsp. cinnamon
4 c. water
2 c. oatmeal

Instructions

1. Arrange the apples, syrup, and cinnamon in the bottom of the slow cooker.
2. Empty the oatmeal and water on top, of the mixture, not stirring.
3. Cook on low for eight to nine hours.
4. Wake up and enjoy your healthy breakfast.

Yields: 3-4 Servings

Pumpkin Oatmeal Breakfast Bars

Enjoy this tasty and healthy treat around Thanksgiving and Christmas. Of course, you can enjoy it anytime!

Ingredients
3 tbsp. maple syrup
2/3 c. coconut sugar
1 ¾ c. canned pumpkin puree
1 tsp. raw apple cider vinegar
1 c. of each:
    -Oat flour
    -Rolled old-fashioned oats
½ tbsp. cinnamon
1 tbsp. pumpkin pie spice
1 t. baking soda
¼ t. salt
1/3 c. pecans

Instructions

1. Add a measured piece of parchment paper into the 7-quart slow cooker. Spray the base of the slow cooker with some cooking oil so that the paper will stick to it.

2. In a large mixing container, combine the vinegar, maple syrup, pumpkin, and coconut sugar. Blend in the oat flour, oats, ¼ cup of pecans, salt, baking soda, pumpkin pie spice, and cinnamon. Mix until well combined into a thick dough.

3. Spread out the batter in the prepared cooker. Sprinkle with the rest of the pecans.

4. Place a lid on the crockpot, to cook on low for one to two hours. Turn off the heat on the cooker and let the bars cook while resting for one hour.

5. Transfer the bars to a wire rack to completely cool.

6. Slice and enjoy!

Yields: 16 Servings

Spiced Granola with Fruit and Nuts

This healthy choice of natural food will help keep you happy and regular. All you need to do is add the ingredients by following the step-by-step instructions, and your slow cooker will do the work.

Ingredients
1 c. nuts (ex. Walnuts, almonds, pecans, etc.)
4 c. old-fashioned rolled oats
¼ c. of each:
    -Chia seeds
    -Sunflower seeds
1 t. ground cinnamon
¼ t. ground of each:
    -Ginger
    -Nutmeg
½ c. melted coconut oil
½ t. kosher salt
¼ c. coconut flakes
½ c. of each:
    -Pure maple syrup
    -Dried cranberries
2 t. vanilla extract

Instructions

1. Thoroughly spray the sides and bottom of a 5-quart slow cooker (or larger).

2. Combine the salt, ginger, nutmeg, cinnamon, sunflower seeds, chia seeds, oats, and pecans.

3. In a separate container, whisk the vanilla, melted oil, and maple syrup together. Add to the ingredients in the crockpot.

4. Secure the lid on the cooker, leaving a slight ¼-inch gap to let steam escape. This opening will prevent the granola from becoming soggy.

Yields: 12 Servings

Scrambled Tofu Breakfast Burrito

The recipe for this burrito is something you never imagined could be so yummy at breakfast. Add a few spices and claim the western spirit with this sensation!

Ingredients
1 pkg. (7 oz.) crumbled tofu
1 ½ c. cooked black beans/15 oz. can
2 tbsp. of each:
    -Cooked onion
    -Minced green pepper
¾ c. water
½ t. ground turmeric
¼ t. of each:
-Smoked paprika
    -Chili powder
    -Ground cumin
To Taste: Salt and pepper
4 whole wheat burrito-sized tortillas
Extras:
    -Salsa
    -Shredded vegan cheese
    -Lettuce
    -Avocado

Instructions

1. Drain and rinse the beans. The night before, add all of the ingredients – omit the extras and tortillas – to the slow cooker. Set the timer for 7-9 hours on the low setting.

2. The next morning, taste, and add pepper and salt if desired.

3. Spoon the mixture onto each of the tortillas. Add all of the garnishes you wish.

4. Serve and enjoy!

Yields: 1 Cup – 4 Tortillas – 2 Servings

Vegan Breakfast Eggs

Enjoy the natural goodness of vegan style eggs. Spice them up just the way you like them with this easy to follow recipe.

Ingredients
2 tbsp. vegan margarine (ex. Earth Balance)
2 pkg. (16 oz. each) extra-firm tofu – packed in water
2 ½ t. nutritional yeast
1 ¼ t. of each:
    -Granulated onion
    -Granulated garlic
1/8 t. turmeric
½ t. black pepper
¾ t. sea salt

Instructions
1. Open the pouches of tofu and drain the water.

2. Use a large skillet, add the margarine, and warm over medium heat.

3. Toss in the pepper and salt over the tofu, along with the turmeric, garlic, and onion. Cook about five minutes – stirring occasionally.

4. Once the water has evaporated, add the yeast, and continue the process until browned.

5. Serve and enjoy.

Yields: 8 Servings

CHAPTER 2

Lunchtime Goodies

Whether you are enjoying brunch or lunch, you are sure to find a mid-day meal to please your taste buds.

Cauliflower Bolognese with Zucchini Noodles

You will just adore the way this vegan Bolognese spices up the cauliflower. You don't get that heavy texture with the consistency of the cauliflower. The combination is so yummy!

Ingredients for the Bolognese

¾ c. diced red onion

1 head cauliflower – cut into florets

2 small minced cloves of garlic

1 tsp dried basil flakes

2 tsp. dried oregano

2 cans (14 oz. each) no salt added – diced tomatoes

¼ tsp. red pepper flakes

½ c. low-sodium vegetable broth

To Taste: Salt and pepper

For the Pasta:

5 large zucchinis

Instructions

1. Combine all of the Bolognese ingredients into the slow cooker.
2. Set the timer for 3 ½ hours on the high setting.
3. When done, mash the cauliflower until the florets break apart.
4. Spoon the mixture over some zucchini noodles.

Yields: 1 Serving

Chinese Barbecued Tofu and Vegetables

This is a recipe sure to please any lunchtime guests!

Ingredients

3 minced garlic cloves

1 package extra-firm tofu – not silken (14 ounces)

1 small minced onion

2 tsp. minced fresh ginger root

¼ cup hoisin sauce

2 tbsp. seasoned rice wine vinegar

8 ounces tomato sauce – no salt added

¼ tsp. vegan Worcestershire sauce

1 tbsp. of each:

    -Spicy brown mustard

    -Low sodium soy sauce

¼ tsp. of each:

      -Five-spice powder

      -Crushed red pepper

2 tsp. molasses

2 tbsp. water

Optional:

      -Salt

      -1/8 t. ground black pepper

Veggies:

2 medium zucchinis – ½-inch cubes

2-3 broccoli – stalks only

½ large green/red bell pepper (one-inch squares)

1 can sliced water chestnuts (8 oz.)

Instructions

1. Slice the tofu into ½-inch chunks and arrange them in towels, pressing lightly to remove the moisture. Slice them into chunks also.
2. Add the tofu to a hot frying pan and cook until browned evenly. Change the temperature on the crock pot to high.
3. Add the tofu to the slow cooker and secure the lid.
4. In the same pan, slowly cook the ginger, garlic, and onions for approximately three minutes. Add the remainder of the ingredients. Heat and stir until bubbling.
5. Empty the sauce over the tofu and mix well. Secure the lid and continue cooking for three hours on high.
6. Trim the broccoli stalks and peel away the outer skin. Cut them into ¼-inch rounds. When the tofu is done, toss in the broccoli and other veggies. Mix well and cover tightly with the lid.
7. Cook for one hour. Enjoy with some brown rice.

Yields: 3-4 Servings

Corn Chowder

This tangy vegan version of the classic recipe will lighten your day when prepared in your slow cooker.

Ingredients

3 c. vegetable broth

2 cans (12 oz.) whole kernel corn

1 large onion

3 potatoes

1 garlic clove

2 red chili peppers

2 tsp. salt

1 tbsp. of each:

-Chili powder

-Parsley flakes

Pinch of black pepper

1 ¾ c. soy milk

¼ c. vegan type margarine

Juice of 1 lime

Instructions

1. Mince the garlic and chili peppers, and dice the veggies.

2. Cook the peppers, garlic onion, potatoes, veggie broth, corn, chili powder, black pepper, parsley, and salt in the slow cooker.

3. Program the timer for 7 hours on the low setting.

4. When done, add the mixture to a blender, filling it only half full. Give the blender a few pulses and continue to puree until creamy smooth.

5. Once everything is pureed, add it along with the margarine and milk back into the crock pot.

6. Set the cooker for one hour on the low setting.

7. Garnish with some lime juice, serve, and enjoy!

Yields: 6 Servings

Florentine Mac and Cheese

Who said you couldn't have Mac and Cheese? You can- vegan style!

Ingredients

1 package frozen (10 ounces) chopped spinach

1 package elbow macaroni

2 tbsp. olive oil

1 can (15.5 ounces) white beans

1 ¾ c. water

½ cup raw cashews

1 chopped medium onion

2 t. fresh lemon juice

Optional: 1 tbsp. white miso paste

Salt to your liking

¼ t. of each:

    -Cayenne pepper

    -Dry mustard

Pinch ground nutmeg

½ c. dry breadcrumbs

Instructions

1. Prepare and drain the spinach. Rinse and drain the beans.

2. Boil the macaroni in salted water for about eight minutes. Drain and dump into a large container. Toss in the spinach.

3. Use a pan over medium heat and warm one tablespoon of the oil. Stir in the onion and continue cooking slowly about five minutes.

4. In a processor/blender, grind the cashews until powdered. Pour one cup of the water and puree until it has a creamy smooth consistency. Blend in the miso, beans, onion, rest of the water, nutmeg, cayenne, mustard, and lemon juice. When smooth, flavor with salt if desired.

5. Pour the creamy sauce over the spinach and macaroni. Toss until combined.

6. Lightly grease the slow cooker. Transfer the goodies to the pot and cook covered for three hours on the low setting.

7. In a small skillet, warm up the oil and bread crumbs. Stir until well coated, about three to four minutes. Set to the side to cool

8. When all components in the recipe are ready; serve, smile, and enjoy.

Yields: 4 Servings

Lasagna Soup

There is nothing like this one to take care of your Italian cravings. It puts new meaning to preparing a soup and pasta luncheon.

Ingredients

4 ½ c. vegetable broth

1 med. onion

¾ c. dried brown lentils

1 t. of each - dried oregano and basil

3 garlic cloves - minced

1 of each (14 oz.):

    -Diced tomatoes

    -Crushed tomatoes

3 cups chopped spinach leaves

8 lasagna noodles

For the Pesto Ricotta

1 c. raw cashews

¼ pound extra-firm tofu

¼ c. unflavored soy/almond milk

To Taste: Pepper and salt

3-4 tbsp. vegan all-natural pesto (available at Wal-Mart)

1 tbsp. lemon juice

Also Needed: Food Processor

Instructions

1. Drain the tofu. Soak the cashews for 4-8 hours, rinse, and drain.

2. Break the noodles into pieces to fit into the cooker.

3. Set the cooker on high. Add the onion, broth, oregano, basil, garlic, and lentils. Stir to blend. Adjust the timer for about two hours. The lentils should be somewhat firm.

4. Add the crushed and diced tomatoes. Stir and cook for two to three more hours on the high setting.

5. Add the spinach and noodles. Give it another stir. Cook until the spinach wilts – usually about 12 minutes will be sufficient. Give it a sprinkle of pepper and salt.

6. *For the Pesto Ricotta*: Add the milk and cashews into a food processor and puree until creamy. Add the tofu, pulsing several times until it has a texture. Blend in the lemon juice, pesto to taste, pepper, and salt.

7. Divide into bowls and provide a dollop of the ricotta.

Yields: 6 Servings

Potatoes Au-Gratin Style

As a vegan, you can still enjoy the benefits of a russet potato in the 'old-time' favorite. Try this for a scrumptious lunch time experience.

Ingredients

3 red russet potatoes

2 cups cauliflower florets

1 cup plain coconut milk

½ c. nutritional yeast

1 tsp. or to taste of pepper, salt, and paprika

Garnish: Turmeric dash

Instructions

1. Omit the potatoes, but blend everything else in a blender or processor.

2. Empty the mixture into the slow cooker, adding a layer of potatoes.

3. Cover it with the sauce, and repeat the layers with the sauce on top.

4. Prepare the cooker for seven to nine hours on the low heat setting.

5. When ready to eat, add a dash of flavor with a bit of turmeric.

Yields: 2-3 Servings

Sloppy Black-Eyed Pea Sandwich

This delicious sandwich is filled full of a tasty pea mixture on an open-faced bun. You can load up on your protein and extra iron with this hearty stew-type meal.

Ingredients for the Morning:

1/6 c. millet

1/3 c. of each:

    -Chopped carrots

    -Dry black-eyed peas

2 c. water

1 minced garlic clove

2 tbsp. minced bell pepper

¼ tsp. liquid smoke

1 tsp. Cajun seasoning

Ingredients for the Evening:

2 tbsp. tomato paste

1 c. minced kale, collards, or your choice

Pepper and salt to your liking

For Serving: 2-3 buns

Instructions

1. Program the timer for seven to nine hours using the low setting.

2. About 30 minutes before the meal is ready for serving, toss in the tomato paste and greens.

3. Sprinkle with the pepper and salt as a garnish along with a little more Cajun seasoning if you want a bit more spice.

4. Serve open-faced and totally devour the masterpiece.

Yield: 2 Cups

Spinach and Artichoke Pasta

With a delicious pasta such as this; the spinach and artichokes are consumed without guilt!

Ingredients

1 package (8 ounces) penne pasta/whole grain fusilli

½ c. raw cashews

1 pkg. (12 ounces each):

   -Frozen flat-leaf spinach

   -Frozen cauliflower florets

1 tbsp. lemon juice

1 can (15 ounces) artichoke hearts – divided (+) ½ c. reserved liquid

¼ c. nutritional yeast

1 t. of each:

   -Minced garlic

   -Dijon mustard

1/8 t. -more or less – black pepper

Optional:

   -Hot sauce

   -Smoked paprika

Instructions

1. Add the cashews to a small dish and cover with hot water. It is best to soak them overnight, but you should soak for a minimum of 15 minutes.

2. Prepare the pasta and spinach. Drain.

3. Use a food processor and add the cashews, cauliflower, 1 cup of artichoke hearts, lemon juice, ½ c. of artichoke liquid. The pepper, salt, mustard, garlic, and nutritional yeast. Process until creamy.

4. Dice up the rest of the artichoke hearts and add them in with the creamy sauce. Blend in the spinach and pasta.

5. For color, add a bit smoked paprika

6. Serve in an 8x8 pan/dish. Bake 15 minutes at 350ºF. Give it a splash of hot sauce for an extra kick.

Yields: 4 Servings

Vegan Pantry Pot Pie

You can make this pie with many ingredients you may already have in the pantry or freezer. It is very flexible with the ingredient choices.

Ingredients for the Stew

2 small garlic cloves

1 small onion

1 large minced stalk of celery

1 pound - frozen vegetables (for ex. Corn, peas, carrots, green beans, etc.)

1 package (10 oz.) sliced mushrooms

1 ½ cups diced tofu/diced potatoes/beans

1 c. water– more or less as needed

2 tbsp. vegan chicken-flavored bouillon –

 Or 1 ½ c. vegetable broth (total of 2 ½ c. liquids)

Pepper and salt to your liking

1 tsp. dried thyme

2 tbsp. flour as needed/thickening

Ingredients for the Biscuits:

1 c. whole wheat/white flour

½ tsp. of each:

Optional: Dried thyme

Salt

3 tbsp. olive oil (maybe less)

½ c almond milk/plain

Instructions the Night Before:
1. If you use the tofu; cube and bake it first. Mince the onions and clove of garlic.
2. Add the cut-up celery, garlic, onion, and tofu/potatoes in an airtight container in the fridge.

Instructions for the Next Morning:

1. Lightly spray the slow cooker.

2. Mix together all of the stew ingredients – omitting the flour for now.

3. Stir and cook for six to eight hours. (Add one to two cups of water, if cooking over 8 hours.)

4. *30-minutes before Serving*: If it is too thin, add a bit of thickening flour. If it is too thick, add a little more water. Taste and adjust the seasonings as you like it.

5. *Make the Biscuits*: Combine all of the components in the biscuit section to form a dough. Roll out the prepared dough to approximately a one-half-inch thickness. Cut into circles with a glass or cutter.

6. Arrange the biscuits on top of the filling. You can either add them one at a time or scoop the dough to cover the entire top of the filling ingredients.

7. Program the cooker to the high setting for 30 additional minutes.

8. *Note*: Bake the tofu 25-30 minutes at 475ºF. Flip it around two or three times until crispy.

Yields: 4 Servings

CHAPTER 3

Dinnertime Recipes

After a long and hard day at work or play, it is always nice to know you will have dinner waiting in your slow cooker.

Butternut Squash Coconut Chili

This butternut squash recipe will change your way of thinking when you think of Chili.

Ingredients
2 c. butternut squash
2 chopped celery stalks
1 small onion
2 carrots
2 med. apples
4 cloves of garlic
1 med. can of each:
    -Chickpeas
    -Black beans
1 can coconut milk low-fat/400 ml
2 t. chili powder
1 t. of each:
    -Ground cumin
    -Dried oregano
2 tbsp. tomato paste
2 c. vegetable broth
To Your Liking: Salt and pepper
Optional: Cooked basmati rice
For the Garnish:

-Shredded unsweetened coconut
-Fresh cilantro, chives, or parsley

Instructions

1. Drain and rinse the beans.
2. Mince the garlic. Peel and chop/dice the onion, carrots, celery, apples, and squash.
3. Add all of the components of the recipe into the slow cooker – omit the garnishes for now.
4. Set the timer for 8 hours on low or 4 to 6 hours on high.
5. Add the salt and pepper about one hour before time to serve.
6. Add chili powder, and cayenne, also as desired.
7. Open the cooker lid the last 45 minutes of the cycle for the chili to thicken.
8. Add a little more broth if it looks dry.
9. Serve with the rice and garnish as desired.

Yields: 8 Servings/ 1 ½ cups each

Italian Eggplant Casserole with Cashew-Tofu Ricotta

It is hard to believe this is Vegan!

Ingredients for the Cashew – Tofu Ricotta
3 garlic cloves
½ c. of each:
Nutritional yeast
Cashews (2 oz.)
Unsweetened nondairy milk
1 pkg. (15.oz.) firm tofu
½ tsp. salt
2 tsp. lemon juice
Pinch of black pepper

Rest of the Ingredients
1 jar (25 oz.) marinara sauce
1 large eggplant/1 ¼ pounds
For Serving: Cooked pasta

Instructions for the Night Before

1. Prepare the ricotta by combining all of the components in the recipe in a blender or processor until smooth.

2. Place in the refrigerator overnight in an airtight container.

Instructions for the Morning

1. Spray the slow cooker with a small amount of spray.

2. Empty 1/3 of the marinara sauce into the pot.

3. Top it off with eggplant slices, ½ of the ricotta, and 1/3 of the sauce.

4. Repeat the layers and dump the remainder of the sauce.

5. Let it cook for six to eight hours on the low setting.

6. If the dish seems a little too soupy, remove the lid and let it cook about 30 minutes to an hour on the high setting.

Yields: 6 Servings

Vegan Style Lasagna

If you have been searching for a 'meatless' choice for lasagna; your search is over! Why not try some of your homemade tomato sauce (see the recipe below).

Ingredients
1 medium of each chopped:
   -Yellow squash
   -Onion
   -Zucchini
1 ½ tablespoons olive oil
2 c. chopped mushrooms
1 medium eggplant (1/2-inch chunks)
2 c. grape or cherry tomatoes
¼ teaspoon red pepper flakes
4 minced cloves garlic
1 teaspoon salt
2 (24-ounce) jars tomato sauce (4 to 5 cups)
½ teaspoon Italian seasonings (thyme, oregano, basil mix)
Package of 12 uncooked lasagna noodles
1 ½ cups shredded vegan cheese:
      -Mozzarella cheese
      - Parmesan cheese
2 cups *Quick Cashew Basil Cheese* (see below)
Optional Garnish: Fresh chopped basil

Cashew Basil Cheese Ingredients:
½ c. almond milk
2 c. raw cashews
¾ t. sea salt
2 t. minced garlic
¼ c. nutritional yeast
1/2 c. (tightly packed) fresh basil
¼ t. pepper
1 ½ tbsp. fresh lemon juice

Instructions

1. Add oil to a pan using the medium heat setting. Toss in the onion, and cook for two to three minutes.
2. Combine the zucchini, mushrooms, eggplant, and squash with the onions and continue cooking for approximately seven minutes.
3. Blend in the salt, tomatoes, red pepper flakes, garlic, and Italian seasonings. Sauté for several minutes or until the veggies are tender.
4. Remove the pan from the heat and add flavoring with more red pepper flakes or salt if desired.
5. Pour 1 ½ cups of the tomato sauce as a base in the slow cooker. Layer the noodles (break to fit), top with 1/3 of the veggie mixture, and top off with the cashew ricotta, with one cup of sauce.
6. Continue the process, alternating and placing the cashew ricotta in the middle layer with ½ of the shredded cheese mixture.
7. The final layer should be with a layer of noodles, sauce, and the remainder of 1 ½ cups of shredded cheese.
8. Cover in the slow cooker for 3½ to 4 hours. Turn off the cooker and set for 15 minutes.
9. Sprinkle with a bit of fresh basil before you serve your hungry family or friends.
10. *Instructions for the Cheese Basil*: Soak the cashews in hot water for a minimum of ten minutes.
11. Combine all of the ingredients until smooth. You can store it safely in the refrigerator for up to five days.

Note: Use caution because overcooking will make the noodles mushy.
Be sure not to overcook because the noodles will become mushy. Watch it closely!

Yields: 6-8 Servings

Quinoa – Black Bean Chili – Cashew Sour Cream

As a vegan, you will soon discover how much you truly love beans and quinoa. This special vegan cashew sour cream will really send your taste buds on a special trip!

Ingredients
½ c. uncooked quinoa
1 can (15 oz.) black beans
2 ¼ c. vegetable broth
¼ c. of each:
    -Green bell pepper
    -Red bell pepper
14 oz. diced tomatoes
2 garlic cloves
½ of 1 onion
1 shredded carrot
2 t. chili powder
½ small chili pepper
1 ½ t. salt
¼ t. cayenne pepper
1 t. of each:
    -Oregano
    -Ground cumin
    -Freshly cracked black pepper
½ c. corn kernels

Ingredients for the Toppings
Shredded carrot
Chopped green onions
Avocado chunks

Ingredients for Vegan Cashew Sour Cream
3-4 tbsp. water
½ c. soaked cashews

½ tsp. fine sea salt
Splash apple cider vinegar
1 tsp. lime juice

Instructions

1. Rinse and drain the beans. Chop the peppers and onion. Shred the carrot.

2. Soak the cashews in water overnight.

3. Pour in the broth, beans, tomatoes, and quinoa into the slow cooker, stirring well to combine.

4. Toss in the carrots, peppers, garlic and onion. Stir well and blend in the rest of the seasonings.

5. Program the crock pot on low for 5-6 hours or 2 ½ -3 hours on the high setting. If you use the lowest setting, check it during the last hour or the high setting, check the last 30 minutes. Add more liquid if needed.

6. Make the Sour Cream: Use a high-speed blender such as the NutriBullet to combine the ingredients until smooth. After 30 seconds, scrape the blender.

7. Serve with some chopped green onions or avocado bits.

Yields: 4-5 Servings

Spinach Marinara Sauce – Vegan Style

This veggie delight is loaded with a tasty sauce right out of the slow cooker. All you need to do is combine the ingredients.

Ingredients
1 chopped onion
¼ c. olive oil
4 minced garlic cloves
1 package (10 oz.) frozen chopped spinach
1 can (4.5 oz.) tomato paste
1/3 c. grated carrot
2 tbsp. of each:
    -Dried basil
    -Salt
    -Dried oregano
1 can (28 oz.) crushed tomatoes with the juices
2 bay leaves
2 ½ tbsp. crushed red pepper
Size of Cooker: 5-Quart

Instructions

1. Thaw the spinach and drain. Drain the mushrooms.
2. Mix all of the ingredients directly into the crock pot.
3. Place the lid on the cooker on the high setting for four hours.
4. Stir and lower the heat setting and cook for one to two more hours.

Yields: 8 Servings

Tomato Sauce

You won't need to purchase a lot of extra sauces when you can make your own using your slow cooker.

Ingredients
½ small chopped onion
10 plum/Roma tomatoes
1 tsp. of each:
    -Minced garlic
    -Ground cayenne pepper
    -Dried basil
    -Salt
    -Dried oregano
    -Black pepper
1 pinch cinnamon
¼ c. olive oil

Instructions

1. Peel and crush the tomatoes and mince the garlic. Toss them into the cooker along with the remainder of the ingredients.

2. Cover with a lid and cook on low for 10-15 hours. The longer they cook, the more flavor will entwine.

Yields: 6 Servings

CHAPTER 4

Snack Time

You can have a little variety for snacks from the Mexican Tacos to the Banana Brown Betty!

Mexican Quinoa Tacos

If it isn't quite time for lunch or dinner; try one of these tacos and share with a few friends.

Ingredients
2 cans (15 ounces each) black beans
1 can (15 oz.) corn
1 can (10 oz.) enchilada sauce
1 can (14.5 oz.) diced tomatoes with juices
1 cup of each:
 -Vegetable broth
 -Quinoa
1.25 oz. package taco seasoning/3 tbsp.
Tortillas – Corn or flour
Toppings:
 -Diced avocado
 -Fresh lime
 -Cilantro
 Also Needed:
 -Fine Mesh Sieve
 -6-Quart Slow Cooker

Instructions

1. Drain and rinse the black beans. Thoroughly rinse the quinoa in the sieve to remove the coating of bitter saponin.

2. In the crock pot, add the broth, undrained tomatoes, taco seasoning packet, drained corn, enchilada sauce, rinsed quinoa, and black beans.

3. Stir until well combined. Place a lid on the cooker for 2 ½ to 4 hours on high.

4. Note: If your cooker tends to get super-hot, it is a good idea to watch the ingredients to make sure they don't get mushy. Don't use the slow temperatures because it will be mushy for longer times.

5. After the quinoa is done, serve on the tortillas with your chosen toppings.

Yields: 6-8 Servings

Puttanesca Pizza

Take it from Oprah; this is so yummy! You know it's healthy with all of the fresh ingredients.

Ingredients for the Dough
½ tsp. of each:
- Salt
- Italian seasoning

1 ½ tsp. instant yeast
1 ½ cups unbleached all-purpose flour
½ cup warm water/as needed
1 tablespoon olive oil

Ingredients for the Sauce
¼ cup of sliced and pitted of each:
- Green olives
- Kalamata olives

½ cup crushed tomatoes
1 tbsp. of each:
- Capers – rinsed and drained
- Chopped fresh flat-leaf parsley

¼ tsp. of each:
- Hot red pepper flakes
- Sugar – vegan approved
- Garlic powder
- Dried Oregano
- Dried basil

Pepper
Optional: ½ c. shredded mozzarella vegan cheese

Equipment Needed:
5-7 – Quart Slow Cooker
Food processor

Instructions

1. *Prepare the Dough*: Lightly grease a large mixing container.

2. Use the food processor to combine the Italian seasoning, salt, flour, and yeast. Add the oil through the feed tube, with the machine running, along with enough water to form a sticky dough ball.

3. Add the dough to a floured surface – kneading for about one or two minutes. Work it into a ball and add to the prepared bowl – flipping to coat the dough with oil.

4. Cover it with a tea towel. Let it rise in a warm space until about doubled in size. Usually, about one hour is sufficient.

5. *In Another Container*: Prepare the sauce by combining both types of the olives, tomatoes, oregano, basil, capers, pepper flakes, garlic powder, sugar, salt, pepper, and parsley.

6. *Prepare the Insert*: Lightly grease the insert and punch down the dough. Arrange it on a floured surface and flatten it to fit into the cooker.

7. Place the dough in the cooker and add the sauce. Drape a kitchen towel between the lid and sauce to prevent condensation gathering on top of the pizza.

8. Cook one hour and forty-five minutes. If you use the cheese; add it after one hour and fifteen minutes and cook another 30 minutes.

Yields: 2 Servings/4 slices as a side dish

White Bean and Garlic Hummus

What snack section would be complete without at least one tasty dip recipe. This one is proclaimed, a Winner!

Ingredients
6 cloves of garlic
2/3 c. dried white beans
¼ c. extra-virgin olive oil
Black pepper and kosher salt if liked
Juice of 1 lemon
Ideal Cooker Size: 3-Quart

Instructions

1. Empty the rinsed white beans into the cooker along with the garlic.

2. Cover the beans with at least two inches of water over the top of the beans. Cook on high for 4 hours on high or 8 hours on the low-temperature setting.

3. Dump the ingredients into a colander to remove the liquid.

4. Add the garlic and beans to a blender. Pour in the juice and olive oil.

5. Puree until creamy.

6. Add a sprinkle of pepper and salt. Enjoy!

Yields: 1 ½ cups

For the Sweet Tooth

This is a recipe you will want to keep close-by for those mid-morning or mid-afternoon slumps.

Banana Brown Betty

Ingredients
½ t. ground cinnamon
1/3 c. pure maple syrup
¼ c. unsweetened almond milk
¼ t. ground of each:
    -Nutmeg
    -Ginger
1/8 t. salt
4 ripened bananas
6 c. cubed white bread
1/3 c. of each:
    -Vegan approved natural sugar
    -Chopped toasted pecans
2 tbsp. rum/brandy/1 tsp rum or brandy extract
Also Needed: 4-quart size slow cooker

Instructions

1. Peel and chop the bananas.

2. Mix the almond milk, syrup, ginger, cinnamon, salt, and nutmeg. Add the breadcrumbs. Stir gently to cover.

3. In another container, mix the vegan type sugar, bananas, pecans, and brandy.

4. Spray the inside of the slow cooker with some cooking oil.

5. Spread ½ of the bread mixture into the bottom, then layer in ½ of the banana concoction, layering until all ingredients are involved.

6. Secure the lid and cook for 1 ½ to 2 hours on the high setting.

7. Serve piping hot.

Yields: 4 Servings

CHAPTER 5

Appetizers to Please

Be prepared with these two crowd pleasers:

Salsa Stuffed Cocktail Tomatoes

Salsa with a bite!

Ingredients for the Dip
¾ c. heaping cashews
½ chopped red bell pepper
2 tbsp. nutritional yeast
2 tsp. onion powder
1 tbsp. tahini
¾ - 1 tsp. sea salt
2 tbsp. lemon juice
1 garlic clove

Ingredients for the Salsa
½ of each one:
    -Red bell pepper
    -Yellow bell pepper
    -Green bell pepper
2 medium tomatoes
Optional: ½ - 1 jalapeno

Ingredients for the Assembly
10-15 cocktail tomatoes

Instructions

1. *Prepare the Dip*: Combine all of the dip components into a high-speed blender along with the red pepper. Lastly, toss in the cashews. Mix until creamy. Place I the fridge to chill.

2. *Make the Salsa*: Cut the tomatoes into quarters and pulse, chopping small. Add to a dish and do the same procedure with the peppers.

3. Use a colander to strain the liquid.

4. *Stuff the Tomato*: Slice the ends off of the tomatoes. Remove the insides.

5. Combine the dip and 2/3 – ¾ of the salsa into each tomato or to your liking.

6. You can also stuff cucumbers the same way.

7. Garnish with some extra salsa.

Yields: 10-15 Tomatoes

Pistachio Crusted Vegan Style Cheese Ball

Be the belle of the party by serving this delicious appetizer on a fancy dish for all your friends.

Ingredients
Juice of 2 limes/2 tbsp.
¼ tsp. each:
    -Pepper
    -Salt
1 c. soaked cashews
1 tbsp. of each:
    -White cooking wine
    -White vinegar
2 garlic cloves
2 tbsp. water
1 sprig of each:
    -Thyme
    -Rosemary
½ - ¾ c. crushed pistachios

Instructions

1. Soak the cashews overnight in the refrigerator in enough water to completely cover them. Drain the water in the morning.

2. Add the cashews to a food processor, and add the rest of ingredients, omitting the pistachio, thyme and rosemary for now.

3. You have made the cheese which is creamy and fully incorporated.

4. Lastly, stir in the thyme and rosemary. Taste and salt if desired.

5. Scoop the cheese mixture into a piece of cheesecloth or a thin tea towel. Arrange it I a strainer and leave it in the refrigerator to drain the liquids overnight.

6. In the morning, take the ball out of the cloth. It should be firm. Smooth the edges and place it into a bowl of pistachios.

7. Roll the ball until it is covered.

8. Enjoy it with some crackers and friends.

Yields: 5-6 Servings

CHAPTER 6

Delicious Desserts

You will surely tempt your taste buds with these yummy treats!

Black Bean Chocolate Pudding

This brings the vegan together with a dairy-free and gluten-free clean eating choice. You will enjoy this recipe with every spoonful.

Ingredients
½ c. almond/coconut/soy milk
¾ c. dried black beans
3 tbsp. cocoa powder
4 tbsp. light blue agave nectar
2 tbsp. coconut /avocado oil
½ large avocado
1 can (14 oz.) coconut full-fat milk
Best Size Cooker: 3-Quart

Instructions

1. Rinse the beans and add them to the crock pot.

2. Over cover the beans with water by about two inches. Place the lid on the cooker on low for eight hours.

3. Empty the liquid off of the beans when they are softened, saving about two cups of the beans.

4. Use a high-powered blender and add the milk along with the beans, blending until creamy. Let the mixture cool off in the refrigerator. Shake the coconut milk in the can for about 30 seconds and add it to the fridge – unopened. It is best to let it set overnight.

5. Empty the cooled beans into the blender.

6. Melt the oil in the microwave about 30 seconds. Stir in the agave nectar and cocoa powder. Scrape this into the blender and add the avocado.

7. Blend everything until creamy soft. It should take 15-30 seconds.

8. Open the can of coconut milk and fold in ½ of the can into the pudding.

9. Save the other half for the pudding topper.

10. Add the pudding to the individual dishes and store until ready to serve.

Yields: 6 Servings

Blueberry Lemon Cake

The natural flavors in this cake will have the neighbors waiting for an invite to taste this wonderful treat.

Ingredients

Dry Ingredients:
¼ tsp. of each:
  -Stevia (+) 1 tsp. agave nectar
  -Baking powder
½ c. whole wheat pastry flour

Wet Ingredients:
¼ c. blueberries
1/3 c. unsweetened nondairy milk
1 tsp. of each:
  -Ground flax seeds mixed with 2 tsp. warm water
  -Olive oil/applesauce/pumpkin puree
¼ tsp. of each:
  -Lemon extract
  -Vanilla extract
½ tsp. lemon zest
Also Needed:
1 1/2 – 2-quart slow cooker
Cooking oil
Parchment paper

Instructions

1. After the prep work, spray the crock pot with cooking oil or line it with some parchment paper if you want to continue oil-free.

2. Combine the dry ingredients and blend in the wet ones.

3. Empty the mixture into the cooker and spread it out evenly.

4. Help absorb some of the condensation by placing a tea towel between the top and cake. Cook for 60-80 minutes. The middle will be solid when touched.

Yields: 4 Servings

Caramelized Apples

This is one of those treats that is tasty whether it is enjoyed, morning – noon – or night.

Ingredients
1 tbsp. lemon juice
1 ½ pounds/5 ½ large apples
½ tsp nutmeg
2 tsp. ground cinnamon
½ - ¾ molasses – to taste
1 ½ tsp. stevia – 3 pkg.
2 tbsp. cornstarch
1 c. apple cider

Instructions

1. Core and slice the apples.

2. Spray the inside of the slow cooker and add the molasses, stevia, nutmeg cinnamon, juice, and apples. Stir it well and mix the cider and starch, pouring it over the apples.

3. Program the crock pot for three to four hours on the low setting. Stir about ½ through the process.

4. Serve with oatmeal, or any other time you want something naturally sweet.

Yields:5 Cups

Slow-Cooked Coconut Raisin Rice Pudding

See if this one can come close to Grandma's recipe.

Ingredients
1 c. of each:
  -Full-fat coconut cream/milk
  -Short-grain rice (ex. Arborio)
1/3 c. raisins
4 c. dairy-free milk – can mix flavors
½ t. ground cinnamon
Pinch of salt
¼ t. ground of each:
  -Cloves
  -Nutmeg
½ t. of each:
  -Vanilla extract
  -Coconut extract
1/3 c. coconut palm sugar

Instructions

1. Combine all of the components – omit the sugar and extracts.

2. Stir and cover for two hours on the high heat setting.

3. Add the vanilla and coconut extract along with the sugar. Stir until dissolved.

4. Serve warm or place in the refrigerator for later.

Yields: 6 Servings

Conclusion

Thank for making it through to the end of Vegan Slow Cooker Cookbook: *Easy Slow Cooker Vegan Recipes to follow.* Let's hope it was informative and provided you with all of the tools you need to achieve your goals of

The next step is to decide which one of the tasty 31 you will try first. Let your friends and family help you choose. Make a list, so you aren't tempted at the market. Gather all of the ingredients and begin the first experiment right away.

If you fail the first try, make the adjustments, and enjoy the experience. Mistakes are the best way to acquire new skills!

Lastly, if you enjoyed this cookbook a review on Amazon will always be appreciated.

Index

Chapter 1: Breakfast Delights

Chapter 2: Lunchtime Goodies

Chapter 3: Dinnertime Recipes

Chapter 4: Snack Time

Mexican Quinoa Tacos
Puttanesca Pizza
White Beans and Garlic Hummus

For the Sweet Tooth

Banana Brown Betty

Chapter 5: Appetizers to Please

Salsa Stuffed Cocktail Tomatoes
Pistachio Crusted Vegan Style Cheese Ball

Chapter 6: Delicious Desserts

Black Bean Chocolate Pudding
Blueberry Lemon Cake
Caramelized Apples
Slow-Cooked Coconut Raisin Rice Pudding

Printed in Poland
by Amazon Fulfillment
Poland Sp. z o.o., Wrocław